SUPERCARRIERS

SUPERCARRIERS

Naval air power in action

Tony Holmes &
Jean-Pierre Montbazet

Published in 1990 by Osprey
Publishing Limited, 59 Grosvenor
Street, London W1X 9DA
Member of the George Philip Group

© Osprey Publishing Limited

British Library Cataloguing
in Publication Data:
Holmes, Tony
    Supercarriers: naval air power
    in action
    1. United States. *Navy* – Aircraft
    carriers
    I. Title II. Montbazet, Jean-
    Pierre 623.82550973

ISBN 0–85045–979–6

Compiled, edited and designed
by Richard and Janette Widdows

Phototypeset in the UK
by Keyspools Ltd
Printed in Hong Kong

[The material in this book previously
appeared in the Osprey Aerospace
publications *Seventh Fleet Super Carriers*
(Tony Holmes), *Super Carriers* (Jean-Pierre
Montbazet) and *World Super Carriers* (Tony
Holmes & Jean-Pierre Montbazet)]

CONTENTS

TITLE PAGES An evocative scene from the hangar deck of the USS *John F. Kennedy* as weak sunlight breaks through to brighten the white-capped ocean.

OPPOSITE The helmet of an electronic warfare officer from VAQ-134 'Garudas' pictured perched on the windmill propeller that energizes the jammer pod via a Garrett AiResearch ram-air turbine on board the EA-6B Prowler.

INTRODUCTION PAGES A radio intercept officer of VF-84 'Jolly Rogers' gives the 'thumbs-up' sign as his pilot prepares to launch their F-14 Tomcat from the USS *Nimitz*.

JEAN-PIERRE MONTBAZET is employed as a journalist by the French television station FR3, living in Paris with his German-born wife Ingrid and their son, Benjamin. Interestingly, Jean-Pierre met Ingrid in London and they were married in the beautiful English city of Bath in 1976.

The publication of this book conveys Jean-Pierre's enthusiasm for naval aviation and his extensive programme of visits to the following US aircraft carriers in the Mediterranean Sea: USS *Forrestal* (CV-59); USS *Dwight D. Eisenhower* (CVN-69); USS *Nimitz* (CVN-68); USS *Coral Sea* (CV-43); USS *America* (CV-66); and USS *Saratoga* (CV-60).

His contribution would not have been possible without the generous help of Captain William A. Rockwell, US naval attaché in Paris, and Philip Brown, press attaché at the US Embassy in Paris and his staff. He would also like to thank the United States Navy, the commanders, officers, press attachés and crews of the CVs for their hospitality and assistance over a considerable period.

TONY HOLMES is currently employed by Osprey Aerospace in London as *Superbase* and technical aviation editor. Born and bred in Western Australia, he made the transition back to the 'mother country', via the USA, in 1988. He has been interested in aviation as long as he can remember and it's a passion instilled in him by his father, also an avid aircraft enthusiast.

He has visited many US Navy vessels but the majority of the photographs in this book were taken on board the USS *Enterprise* (CVN-65) and USS *Carl Vinson* (CVN-70) while both carriers were in the Indian Ocean, and the USS *Ranger* (CV-61) in 1987 when she was cruising in the Western Pacific.

Taking the pictures featured in the publication would not have been possible without the generous help of Glynis Johns and James Faulkner Channing at the US Consulate in Perth, Lieutenant Bob Anderson, Seventh Fleet Public Affairs in the Philippines, Captain (retired) Ross Underhill USN, the Public Affairs Officers at Atsugi, and the guides who showed the author around the CVs. Finally, Tony would like to thank the commanders, officers and crews of the *Enterprise, Carl Vinson, Ranger* and NAF Atsugi for their warm hospitality and valued assistance during his visits.

[Photograph by Michelle Garside]

INTRODUCTION

A glance across a packed flight deck emphasizes the potency of the modern air wing. At the tip of the Navy's 'sword' is the world's premier fighter-interceptor, the Grumman F-14 Tomcat. Two squadrons and anything up to 26 F-14s form the air superiority umbrella for the carrier, the remainder of the air wing and other vessels supporting the battle-group. Working closely with the F-14 to form an all-seeing Grumman partnership is the E-2C Hawkeye, a single squadron of four aircraft providing the long-range 'eyes and ears' for the air wing's fighters.

Rivaling the Tomcat pilots of late as the dog-fighting masters are the strike/fighter crews who fly the formidable McDonnell-Douglas F/A-18 Hornet. A true all-rounder in both the fighter and attack stakes, the Hornet has further boosted the capability of the modern air wing. Thirty Hornets split evenly between two squadrons are usually to be found aboard the large US carriers, although the smaller and older *Midway* class vessels cruise with three squadrons of F/A-18s deployed.

Slowly disappearing from the crowded carrier decks is the venerable Vought A-7E Corsair II, the light attack aircraft that is being replaced by the Hornet. A combat veteran of Vietnam, Grenada and the Lebanon, the A-7 still features prominently within the pages of this book–a fitting salute to an aircraft that has given the US Navy sterling service for over two decades.

The heavy attack element of the carrier force is provided by a single squadron of the ageless Grumman A-6 Intruder. An aircraft that can deliver a pinpoint punch in any weather, 24 hours

a day, the Intruder has been a vital part of US naval aviation since the mid-1960s and should remain so through to the next century.

The distinction of operating the most expensive aircraft goes to the electronic warfare squadron, this specialist group flying four Grumman EA-6B Prowlers in support of other air wing assets. Costing roughly $60 million a piece, the Prowler is packed with radar sensor equipment – devices which allow the aircraft's four-man crew to perform electronic wizardry with an enemy's radar and detection gear.

One of the largest aircraft to be found on a carrier deck today is the Lockheed S-3A Viking, a state-of-the-art anti-submarine warfare platform of immense capability. Designed specifically for carrier operations, the portly Viking is flown by a solitary unit within the air wing, ten examples usually comprising a squadron.

The final type to be regularly spotted aboard ship is the venerable Sikorsky SH-3H Sea King, a large helicopter with a long history. Tasked with the ASW role, the Sea King is more regularly used as the plane-guard during carrier operations. No fixed-wing aircraft will be cleared for launch on the carrier unless a Sea King is hovering off the port beam ready to respond should a crew get into difficulties. A single squadron of six SH-3s is the typical air wing complement.

All of these types are graphically covered in the following pages, supported by several other types only recently retired from the sea-swept decks of US Navy carriers. Classics like the F-4 Phantom II, the ultimate Navy fighter of the 1960s and early 1970s, and the AV-8 Harrier, the first vertical take-off and landing military jet ever flown operationally from a carrier deck, are illustrated performing at sea in all their former glory.

A photographic tribute not only to naval aviators but to naval aviation as a whole, this book places you on the rolling deck as the mighty force of the US Navy goes about its business.

FLIGHT DECK

The flight deck of an aircraft carrier is no place for the faint-hearted or work-shy. Side-stepping jet-blast, the deadly suction of intakes, whirling propellers or busy tow tractors and ducking under the wings of launching aircraft either becomes instinctive or you become a statistic. On a deck with no railings – not even a handhold – positional awareness and good judgment are essential. At every level of operations safety is a way of life. The precarious job of marshaling large, bulky combat aircraft around a crowded and pitching carrier deck also involves considerable skill – and much forward planning.

LEFT Ordnance men on duty. The color of a deck crewman's jersey, life-jacket and helmet tells everyone around him what kind of job he does.

FLIGHT DECK

Below and Top right A Grumman A-6E TRAM of VMA(AW)-121 'Green Knights' prepares to launch from the USS *Ranger*. The catapult crewman is signaling the all-clear to the shooter. Once sufficient pressure has been built up in the enormous catapult mechanism one level below the flight deck, the shooter relays this message to the pilot. The pilot then confirms he is all set for launch through the familiar 'thumbs-up' signal, the shooter then squeezing the trigger which fires the catapult.

Bottom The shooter and his fellow catapult
crewmen going about their daily business on *Ranger*.

BELOW Armed with practice bombs, an A-6E
Intruder of VA-35 'Black Panthers' needs a firm
shove to get it into the right spot before starting up.

BELOW When the catapult officer drops his knee and points down the deck, the 'shooter' presses a button which signals the order to fire to the catapult controller a deck below.

RIGHT A Grumman EA-6B Prowler electronic warfare aircraft of VAQ-134 'Garudas' is shot from one of the waist catapults on the USS *Carl Vinson*. The aircraft's leading edge slats are drooped fully to give the wing as much 'bite' as possible.

BELOW Armed with a mix of Phoenix, Sidewinder and Sparrow air-to-air missiles (AAMs), a Grumman F-14 Tomcat of VF-1 'Wolfpack' is guided onto bow catapult one aboard the USS *Ranger*. Thanks to the powerful steam catapult, even if the Tomcat's engines failed during the shot it would only leave the deck five knots slower, giving the crew enough time to eject.

BELOW 'The Maestro': a catapult officer conducting flight operations on the USS *Ranger*. This man's job is vital to the success of all flight deck ops, since he is charged with guiding the large cumbersome aircraft onto the catapult shuttle. The time factor between launches is kept to a minimum, a lot of the immediate strike capability on offer from the air wing being lost if this man is not proficient. The downward visibility from the lofty perch of an aircraft is minimal and the pilot relies heavily on the man in front, 'conducting', for his directions.

LEFT Each squadron on a carrier has its own landing signal officer (LSO), a veteran pilot who guides his fellow aviators down the approach. If a pilot is flying his aircraft nicely on the glideslope and sticking to the centreline, the LSO will mainly confine his patter to reassurance; if a pilot isn't getting it right, the LSO will feed him corrections and sort things out; if the pilot really screws up, or if the deck becomes obstructed, the LSO will give him a wave-off and send him around again.

BELOW LEFT Two hook-up men inspect one of the arrester cables on the USS *Forrestal*. They prepare aircraft for launch and secure them to the catapults.

BELOW Green-shirted maintenance men peer under an unlatched access panel on a Tomcat prior to fixing a minor avionics problem.

RIGHT Leading edge flaps are vitally important on any carrier aircraft as they help to slow down and control the machine before it lands. This is especially true of the Corsair which, because of its relatively small wing area, lands at about 140 knots. Here, greenshirts are inspecting the flap hydraulic actuators on Corsair 158016 of VA-97 'Warhawks'.

BELOW *Nimitz*'s Oshkosh fire truck stands by in front
of the island. Fire is the carriers' greatest enemy.

BELOW Firemen relax on the roof of a different fire truck on the USS *Forrestal*.

BOTTOM These newer, smaller all-purpose fire tractors are currently replacing the larger Oshkosh fire trucks on US Navy carriers. This is one of several such vehicles embarked on the USS *Carl Vinson*.

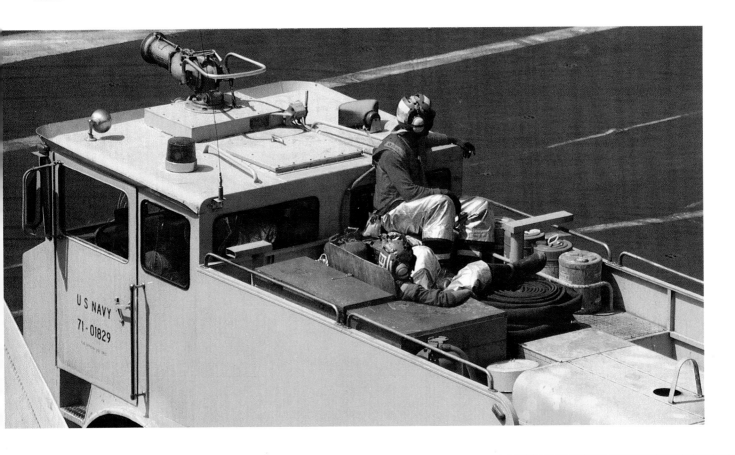

FLIGHT DECK

A 'mule' tow tractor hauls an E-2C Hawkeye to its
parking spot on the USS *Coral Sea* as she lays at
anchor in the Bay of Cannes in the South of France.
Mules are yellow tractors used to move aircraft on the
flight and hangar decks.

LEFT A tow tractor (short variety) with a load of wheel chocks.

BELOW A 'hopper' or 'mule' goes about its business as it tows a recently retrieved aircraft back to the parking area on the stern of *Carl Vinson*.

RIGHT Mule on the move. In addition to their towing tasks, the larger tractors like this one can carry a generator on the back for starting aircraft.

BELOW RIGHT The cockpit of tow tractor number 14. A rough antislip coating decorates the top of the vehicle.

The next job for this tow tractor aboard the USS *Forrestal* is to haul away the EA-6B Prowler of VAQ-130 'Zappers' parked in the background.

BELOW A mule driver takes five on the *Saratoga*. A blue jacket with a stenciled 'T' entitles you to drive your own machine and enjoy the luxury of being able to sit down most of the time.

BOTTOM Two F-14 Tomcats of VF-84 'Jolly Rogers' on the *Nimitz*. The airplane on the left is ready to be towed out: the plane captain in the front cockpit is there to work the toe brakes as the aircraft makes its

way across the deck. Every aircraft in the air wing has a plane captain (identified by his brown jacket) who is responsible for ensuring the serviceability and cleanliness of the machine under his charge.

BELOW The stabilizer mechanism from an A-6E of VA-145 'Swordsmen', shore-based at NAS Whidbey Island, Washington, gets attention aboard the USS *Ranger*.

FLIGHT DECK

BELOW Ordnance men with the ammunition loading system they use to feed shells into the magazine of the Vulcan M61 rotary cannon used by the A-7 and F-14. These men also handle and load bombs, missiles, torpedoes, sensors and jammers.

ABOVE Guiding their deadly load over the grimy deck of *Carl Vinson*, redshirts push along the hefty weight of six Mk 83 1000 lb bombs. The fuse mechanisms are carried by the officer behind them and screw into the nose of each bomb.

LEFT An armorer from VA-95 'Green Lizards' works over the pop-out fins which retard the Mk 92 Snakeye bomb he's soon to prime on an A-6. It's vital that the bombs are fitted securely to the triple ejector racks (TERs) because the forces exerted on the aircraft during launch and recovery can wrench loose ordnance from the racks – with potentially disastrous results.

BELOW The retarding fins of the Mk 92 Snakeye are clearly seen as a redshirt guides 2000 lb of high explosive towards waiting A-6 and A-7 strike aircraft.

FLIGHT DECK

BELOW A plane captain inspects the rear Martin-Baker GRU-7A ejection seat of a Tomcat during a serviceability check.

RIGHT Scrubbing the decks is an old naval tradition but it's just as important today; after a sustained period of flight operations the deck becomes slick with vented jet fuel, lubricants and hydraulic fluid.

ABOVE Sorting out the 'black boxes', containing the plane's avionics, in an A-7E.

RIGHT A crewman in combat fatigues and *Tarawa* sweatshirt finds a handhold on the tailcone radar warning receivers during a check on an AV-8C Harrier.

ABOVE EA-6B Prowler, side number 607, of VMAQ-2 'Playboys' moves slowly towards the parking lot after landing aboard *Saratoga*. The latest ICAP-2 standard Prowlers had recently entered service when this picture was taken in August 1984, fitted with a digital power management system to maximize their effectiveness against a cohesive range of frequency agile emitters. In addition to the pilot, three crew are needed to operate the system.

A maintenance man perches on the tail section of a
Sikorsky SH-3H Sea King helicopter of HS-3
'Tridents' aboard *Saratoga*.

BELOW At dawn the flight deck of a carrier is a hive of activity. This is a scene aboard the 'Starship' *Enterprise* as the groundcrews go about readying the aircraft for the day's first flight operations. The AIM-9L Sidewinder AAMs on the right will shortly be fitted to the Vought A-7E Corsairs of VA-94 'Mighty Shrikes'.

RIGHT Taking a break from their work inside this Grumman E-2 Hawkeye airborne early warning (AEW) aircraft of VAW-114 'Hormel Hawgs', the brown-shirted plane captain and green-shirted maintenance man peer out of the overhead cockpit windows. It appears that the 'Hawg' emblem is too conspicuous for the Navy's liking and the squadron have been told to scale this piggy down. Never!

RIGHT The plane captain polishes off the protective coating on the windshield of the CAG's E-2C (BuNo 161344). The receivers underneath the hinged nose cone form part of the Litton AN/ALR-73 passive detection system (PDS), which can detect hostile electro-magnetic emitters at great distances without giving away the presence or position of the eavesdropping Hawkeye.

BELOW Replenishment at (Coral) Sea. The big nuclear carriers come with several years of fuel, but older oil-burning ships such as *Coral Sea* must rendezvous with a fueler to 'top up' for RAS. Regular ship-to-ship transfusions of jet fuel for the JP5 guzzling Air Wings are needed by all carriers. Note the ordnance multiple ejector racks (MERs) stored in the 'pit' to the right.

RIGHT Fueling time for the Harriers of VMA-513 aboard the USS *Tarawa*.

BELOW Aircraft are refueled by 'grapes' – men wearing purple jackets. Here a Corsair is receiving its fill of JP5 through the pressure hose plugged in near the landing gear. The airplane is carrying an AIM-9L Sidewinder (fitted with its protective nose cap) on its port missile rail.

BELOW Refueling an F-14 Tomcat. This 'grape' seems happy enough in his work – despite the miserable weather.

LEFT An F-14 Tomcat of VF-41 'Black Aces' in an experimental low-visibility scheme ready to be towed away past light gray colleagues on the *Nimitz*.

BELOW A pair of VF-2 'Bounty Hunters' head up a line of Intruders parked on the bow of the *Ranger*. While the Intruder folds, the wing of the F-14 is equipped with an 'oversweep' facility to maximize parking space – a crucial consideration with 90 or more aircraft jockeying for space on and below the flight deck.

BELOW EA-6B Prowler, side number 610, of VAQ-130 'Zappers' is flanked by an S-3A Viking and (nearest camera) an A-7E Corsair as maintenance work proceeds aboard the USS *Forrestal* (CV-59).

LEFT A-7E Corsair of VA-97 'Warhawks' spotted in the tie-down area on the deck of CVN-70 USS *Carl Vinson* in 1986.

BELOW F-14s of VF-111 'Sundowners' spring into action on *Carl Vinson* at the start of an air defence mission.

LEFT An S-3A Viking of VS-38 'Red Griffins' unfolds its wings before being launched from the USS *Ranger*. The moment arm on the wing-fold hinge must be considerable.

ABOVE A VA-82 Corsair pilot goes around for some more approach practice after a 'touch and go' landing on the *Nimitz*. 'Salt One', the Grumman C-1A Trader in the foreground, was assigned to *Nimitz* as a COD (carrier on-board delivery) aircraft when this picture was taken in January 1983.

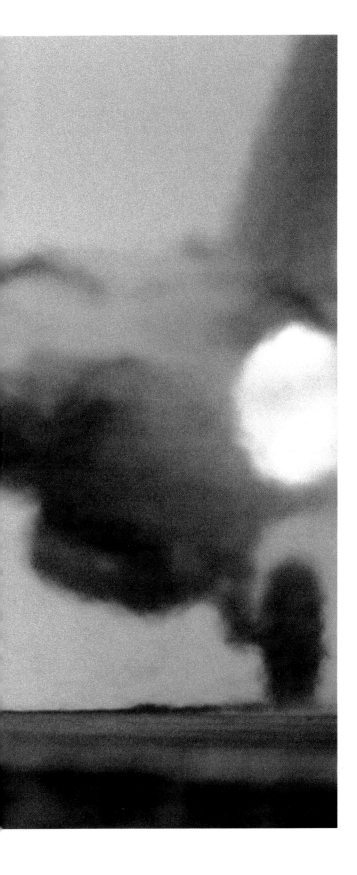

TOMCAT 'Anytime baby'

The F-14 Tomcat is still probably the best long-range air superiority fighter ever built. It's got so many design features that other combat aircraft look positively austere by comparison.

Tomcat is a Mach 2+, two-seat, twin-engined, twin-finned, variable geometry (with auto-sweep) aircraft with more missile muscle than any other existing fighter. With its unique combination of the Hughes AWG-9 radar system and AIM-54 Phoenix missiles, the Tomcat can engage simultaneously six targets flying at heights varying between 50 feet and 80,000 feet, and traveling at speeds of up to Mach 2.8 at a range in excess of 100 miles – a capability unmatched by any other fighter in the world.

The US Navy intends to operate a maximum of 24 Tomcat squadrons and production is expected to pass the 800-mark in the 1990s. A total of 49 F-14s have been modified to carry a centreline TARPS (tactical airborne reconnaissance pod system), and these aircraft have replaced the RA-5C Vigilante and RF-8G Crusader.

LEFT AND OVERLEAF Afterburner! Riding 40,000 lbs thrust from its two Pratt & Whitney TF30-P-412A turbofan engines, F-14A Tomcat side number 212 of VF-32 'Swordsmen' blasts off from one of the USS *John F. Kennedy's* waist catapults. Note the marked (but not full) upward deflection of its all-moving tailplane as the catapult shot begins, and the differential action as the Tomcat climbs away.

Top The 'Swordsmen' from VF-32 were among the first US Navy Atlantic Fleet squadrons to become operational on Tomcats. With VF-14's 'Tophatters' they achieved a 100 per cent kill rate during missile-firing exercises on their first Mediterranean cruise aboard the USS *John F. Kennedy* in 1975, although this sequence of a 'Swordsmen' Tomcat shooting the bow cat from *JFK* dates from 1986.

Above Tomcat's snout. Note the muzzle of the General Electric M61A1 Vulcan 20 mm gun in the port side and the chin-mounted Northrop television camera sight (TCS), which can scan a 30-degree field of view, tracking targets even under high G conditions and giving the backseat radar intercept officer (RIO) a magnified image of the 'bogey' for identification. The Hughes AN/AWG-9 radar can track up to 24 targets simultaneously (and attack six of them), and is capable of detecting fighter-sized aircraft at ranges up to 195 miles.

LEFT The F-14A is launched in the 'kneeling' position with the nosewheel strut compressed. As the catapult completes its stroke the energy in the compressed strut is released, pitching the nose of the aircraft up into the correct flying attitude.

BELOW The 'Swordsmen' of VF-32 have retained some of their bright heraldry, despite the move towards toned-down low-visibility markings on US Navy carrier aircraft in recent years.

BELOW, INSET A Sidewinder and Sparrow-armed Tomcat of VF-213 'Black Lions' about to trap aboard the USS *Enterprise*. Piles of yellow wheel chocks are in the foreground.

ABOVE In the groove: hook down, gear down, slattery and flappery extended, this 'Black Lions' Tomcat is poised to make a perfect 'trap' on *Enterprise*.

ABOVE RIGHT The sun is low in the sky as a VF-51 'Screaming Eagles' Tomcat prepares to launch on the first mission of the day. The aircrews' tinted visor becomes essential in such situations.

RIGHT Toting an AIM-9L Sidewinder on the outer glove pylon, a VF-51 Tomcat, side number 101, BuNo 160675, taxies past two A-7E Corsairs and towards the bow cats. This particular aircraft has had its overall matt gray finish touched up with a bluish shade of a similar color. Depending on the light conditions at the time, these low-viz Tomcats can appear to be painted in one of several shades.

F-14A TOMCAT

RIGHT Seconds away from the shot, a kneeling white shirt confirms that the engine nozzles are wide open, a sure sign the Pratt & Whitney TF30 turbofans are each producing their maximum advertised thrust of 20,900 lb. The job done by the raised deflector shield can be seen clearly as the heat produced by the engines is blown up into the air.

BELOW The flight deck crew look on as a Tomcat from VF-2 'Bounty Hunters' prepares to launch from waist catapult four on the USS *Ranger*.

ABOVE The huge bulk of the F-14 is emphasized by this low-down angle, but it's a beautiful beast! The muzzle blast trough for the 20 mm M61 Vulcan gun can be seen immediately below the nose code. Also visible on this VF-111 'Sundowners' machine is the undernose Northrop TVSU (television sight unit) which gives the RIO a magnified image of a 'bogey' about nine miles distant to identify it visually before commencing an attack.

RIGHT Power personified: a VF-51 Tomcat roars down the deck of *Carl Vinson*.

BELOW A flight deck crewman guides the Tomcat onto the launch rail; the catapult shuttle used on the previous launch is traveling up the rail behind him and will soon be attached to the aircraft's nosewheel leg. Note they heavy weathering on the wing due to the wing glove sealing plates rubbing along the surfaces every time sweep is selected. The 'swing wing' confers Mach 2-plus performance and 'dogfight' manoeuvrability across a broad spectrum of speeds and altitudes. The 'Screaming Eagles' have been equipped with the F-14 since the unit pensioned off its F-4 Phantom IIs in 1978. VF-51 have enjoyed a longer period of continuous service in the Pacific than any other US Navy fighter squadron, and originally flew Curtiss F6C-4 biplanes as VF-3S 'Striking Eagles' back in 1928.

Right This F-14 from VF-51 'Screaming Eagles' is certainly in good hands! In the front seat is the squadron's commanding officer, Commander Jim Robb, and the RIO in back for this mission is CAG (carrier air group commander) Captain Lyle 'Ho-Chi' Bien. The mottled appearance of the paint below the canopy is interesting.

ABOVE Back in July 1983, VF-111 'Sundowners' were still giving their F-14s the full sharkmouth treatment. This example, side number 207, is also pictured opposite.

LEFT Once a distinguishing feature proudly worn by VF-111, the sharkmouth has disappeared from all their F-14s. Well, almost: this set of gnashers decorated the TVSU bullet of Tomcat '211', BuNo 161144.

ABOVE Its canopy covered in protective polish, this Tomcat is wearing a curious blend of low-viz national insignia, an overall light gray paint scheme and the traditional blood red and white fin and sharkmouth so long associated with VF-111.

RIGHT The CAG's Tomcat features a small Superman motif under the front cockpit. Nicknamed 'Super CAG' because of his high rank, Captain Ron Zlatoper is attached to VF-111 besides being the commander of Air Wing 15.

Although the F-14 first flew two decades ago, in December 1970, only now is the A model's replacement being designed and tested. The new F-14D is the tangible result of pointed advice from seasoned Tomcat fliers. 'There was an incredible amount of growth potential in the basic F-14A aircraft. The F-14D embodies all of the recommended improvements.' So says Lieutenant Commander Kal 'Wrecker' Felt, a VF-51 Tomcat pilot. Perhaps the most important of these from the pilot's standpoint are the new General Electric F110 turbofans. In the current F-14A the pilot has to 'fly the engine' because the TF30 powerplant is vulnerable to flame-outs and surges in violent combat manoeuvres; but the F110 will enable the pilot to slam the throttles wide open without fear throughout the Tomcat's entire flight envelope, especially in the high angle of attack/low speed region. Rated at 29,000 lbs in afterburner, the F110 is also much more powerful and will enable the aircraft to take off in military power (i.e. maximum thrust without afterburning) from a carrier deck as a matter of routine..

BELOW Looking a good deal smarter than its drab brothers, Tomcat '203' (BuNo 160694) proceeds to its allocated catapult. The crew are wearing highly stylized bonedomes decorated with the famous sunray motif of VF-111.

ABOVE A Tomcat driver from VF-14 'Tophatters' aboard USS *John F. Kennedy* (CV-67). The crews spend as long as possible below decks in the comfort of the squadron ready room before strapping on their G-webbing, donning their survival vests and fitting into their suitably decorated bonedomes. Going on cruise with an operational Tomcat squadron is the culmination of almost three years' training for a raw F-14 crew. When back at base the squadrons fly as hard in all manner of exercises against other Navy units, as well as Air Force and Canadian Armed Forces squadrons. Nevertheless, no amount of land-based training can provide a naval aviator with the same experience as a WestPac or Atlantic cruise.

F-14A TOMCAT

BELOW Tomcat in a trap. The target wire is number three of four. Aiming for the early wires can be hazardous if the aircraft gets too low, risking a deck strike; too high, even by a foot, and it's a 'bolter' – a go around for another pass. This F-14 has just been brought to the usual violent, harness jerking halt by the arrester cable. Note the nosewheel leg fully compressed by deceleration, the extended dorsal airbrake and smoke from the engines as the pilot anticipates the 'trap' and pushes the throttles to military power in case of a bolter.

RIGHT Parking is always a problem on carriers, but it's eased by the fact that the F-14 is equipped with an 'overwrap' facility.

BOTTOM A 'Tophatter' trails his hook along the deck of *John F. Kennedy*.

BELOW, INSET Step aboard, but better ask the CAG first. This is the Commander Air Wing's personal F-14A from VF-213 'Black Lions' aboard the USS *Enterprise*.

BELOW A 'Fighting Aardvarks' F-14A from VF-114 aboard the *Enterprise*. Note the AIM-9M Sidewinder air-to-air missile mounted on the starboard outboard wing glove stores station.

F-14A TOMCAT

BELOW F-14A Tomcat from VF-2 'Bounty Hunters',
still retaining high-visibility stars 'n' bars and stencil
marks, awaits a cat shot on the USS *Ranger*. VF-2
was one of the first operational squadrons to receive
Tomcats, commissioning at NAS Miramar,
California on 14 October 1972.

BELOW, INSET Night bolter. Deck landing is a heart-quickening business at the best of times, but night traps are when carrier pilots really earn their flight pay. Here a Tomcat misses the wire (note the sparks from the arrester hook striking the deck) and 'bolters' for another try.

BELOW What big teeth you have: VF-1 'Wolfpack'
F-14A side number 105 aboard USS *Ranger*, seeming
to dwarf a neighboring Viking.

BELOW, INSET Open gun and magazine bays display the Tomcat's six-barrel General Electric M61A1 Vulcan rotary cannon and ammunition drum for 675 rounds of 20 mm. To avoid the possibility of spent ammunition cases being ingested into the Tomcat's large engine intakes – here protected with what appear to be makeshift covers of camouflage material – empty cases are returned to the drum after being extracted from the gun breech.

LEFT F-14A, side number 210, of VF-103, launches from *Saratoga*. The Tomcat's combination of Hughes' AWG-9 pulse-Doppler radar and Phoenix/Sparrow/Sidewinder missiles give it an unrivaled capability against a range of threats, from lightweight fighters to long-range bombers and cruise missiles. Tomcat has successfully destroyed multiple targets at ranges in excess of 100 nm with Phoenix missiles, while an internal 20 mm M61 Vulcan cannon with 675 rounds is used to hose-down targets at very close range – but winning the outer air battle (OAB) is what really counts, zapping those bombers *before* they launch nuclear-tipped cruise missiles at the battlegroup.

BELOW Another F-14A Tomcat, this time side number 201 of VF-103 'Sluggers', prepares to launch from one of Super Sara's' waist catapults during inclement Mediterranean weather. Its inconspicuous markings and low-profile national insignia blend in with the low-visibility paint job.

LEFT VF-103 'Sluggers' use a light gray scheme on their F-14s, but VF-74 'Be-Devilers' prefer overall blue gray. These Tomcats are being readied for flight aboard the USS *Saratoga* (CV-60) in August 1984.

RIGHT With a combined total of over 40,000 lb of glowing white thrust blasting from the nozzles of its Pratt & Whitney TF30 turbofans, an F-14 is launched from *Saratoga*. The US Navy will begin to take delivery of the upgraded F-14D from 1990. General Electric F110 turbofans each rated at 29,000 lb (13,150 kg) will replace the TF30s, and the new aircraft will also feature the Hornet's AYK-14 central computer, a Honeywell laser-gyro INS (inertial navigation system), multi-function cockpit displays and a 30 inch (760 mm) fuselage extension to house an additional 2000 lb of fuel. The F-14D will be fitted with the JTIDS (joint tactical information distribution system) datalink and it's also expected to get a new missile, the AIM-120 AMRAAM.

BELOW Directed by a flight deck crewman (identified by his yellow garb), a VF-74 'Be-Devilers' Tomcat lines up for launch from a bow cat on *Saratoga*.

BELOW RIGHT Even on the big CVN supercarriers deck space is always at a premium with 90 aircraft aboard. 'Spotting' the aircraft, particularly during flying operations, demands the skills of a champion jigsaw puzzlist, though interlocking Tomcats – seen here aboard the USS *John F. Kennedy* – is made easier by an oversweep feature which enables its variable-geometry wings to be swept to 75 degrees, overlapping the tailplanes. The F-14's maximum in-flight sweep is 68 degrees.

F-14A TOMCAT

BELOW AND RIGHT After engaging full afterburner on both engines, an F-14 of VF-213 'Black Lions' is launched amid a shower of steam and heat. The aircraft's proximity to the catapult crew is noteworthy.

BOTTOM 'Thumbs-up' from the RIO (radar intercept officer) in the back seat as he and the pilot prepare to withstand the 'kick' of a catapult launch. VF-84 'Jolly Rogers' still wore colorful squadron markings when this picture was taken back in January 1983.

LT SCOTT KINGSLEY

TOP LEFT Grumman F-14A Tomcat of VF-41 'Black Aces' on the flight deck of the USS *Nimitz* (CVN-68). The shuttle traveling along the catapult track will be attached to the nosewheel strut of the aircraft. When this procedure is completed, the catapult will be ready to 'fire'. In August 1981, the 'Black Aces' splashed two Libyan Sukhoi Su-22s into the Gulf of Sidra.

LEFT Tomcats of VF-33 'Black Star' and VF-102 'Diamondbacks' tightly packed on the rear of *America*'s flight deck.

TOP A VF-41 Tomcat gets airborne from *Nimitz*. Deflector shields are raised to protect men and machines from the heat and blast of each launch.

ABOVE An F-14A Tomcat of VF-41 'Black Aces' successfully engages one of the four arrester cables strung across the deck of *Nimitz*. Take-off thrust is selected at touchdown to ensure that if the pilot lands a little long and misses the wires, or the tailhook hops over them, he has plenty of power to make a safe go-around for another try.

F-14A TOMCAT

An RIO (radio intercept officer) climbs into the rear cockpit of a VF-74 Tomcat. The fold-out steps strategically placed in the F-14's fuselage allow the crew to climb aboard without having to resort to using cumbersome ladders. The RIO is usually the first to strap into the Tomcat, priming his radar and punching in the navigational co-ordinates, leaving the pilot to complete the pre-flight walkaround at deck level. Contrary to popular belief, RIOs are not failed pilots; they are highly trained individuals who choose to occupy the back office from the start, 'RIO school' being based at Pensacola, Florida. Several years ago

RIOs were given the opportunity to transition
forward into the front seat – a programme which was
well received at squadron level but which is no longer
being run.

BELOW Once a fine looking squadron who wore their black and orange colors with pride, all the members of VF-114 'Fighting Aardvarks' feel sad that the low-viz grays have come into vogue. This F-14 is seen in January 1983 sitting proudly beneath the island on the USS *Enterprise*.

RIGHT The colorful twin-tailed lion and piercing blue rudder speckled with gold stars was once a feature of the Tomcats flown by VF-213 'Black Lions'.

CENTRE RIGHT Looking a bit faded and perhaps knowing he is soon to swap his proud orange coat for an inconspicuous gray one, this small 'Fighting Aardvark' Tomcat has cause to feel a little pale.

BOTTOM RIGHT The current tail markings of VF-1 'Wolfpack' and VF-2 'Bounty Hunters'.

ABOVE Tomcat tails. From left: VF-74 'Be-Devilers' from USS *Saratoga*, VF-102 'Diamondbacks' and VF-33 'Tarsiers' from USS *America*, VF-142 'Ghostriders' from USS *Dwight D. Eisenhower*'.

LEFT VF-84 Tomcat at the end of the glide path and poised for a perfect touchdown on *Nimitz*. Red-shirted ordnance men know what a good approach looks like – no sign of anything abnormal so no sweat.

BELOW From zero to 160 knots in 165 feet: a VF-84 Tomcat sporting the 'skull and crossbones' of the 'Jolly Rogers' clears the bow of *Nimitz*.

F-14A TOMCAT

BELOW An F-14A Tomcat of VF-103 'Sluggers' taxies on the flight deck of *Saratoga* before being launched into the sunset.

BELOW AND INSET White heat from the afterburner of a VF-14 'Tophatters' F-14 sears the jet blast deflector (JBD) on the deck of USS *John F. Kennedy* at the start of a night cat shot. Glowing green strips on the nose, wingtips and aft section are 'tape light' panels to aid station keeping on night formation flying.

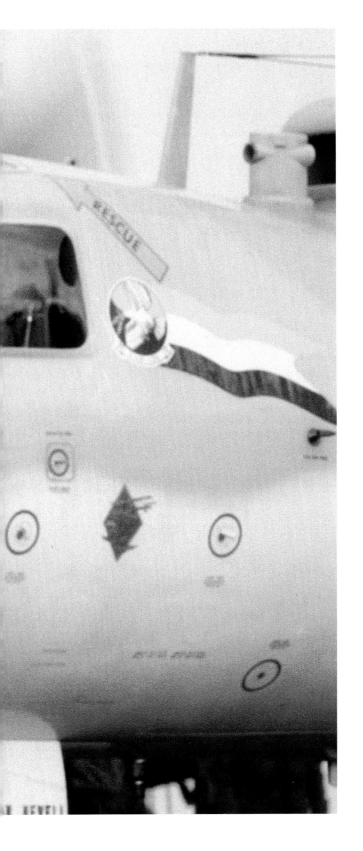

HAWKEYE
Aerial
detective

The role of Grumman's E-2C Hawkeye is to provide the carrier battlegroup with over-the-horizon airborne early warning surveillance. The 'MiniWACS' AN/APS-125 search radar (AN/APS-139 on post-1983 production, and steadily being retrofitted throughout the fleet) can detect targets as small as a cruise missile up to 155 nautical miles away, fighters at 200 nm or more, and can track as many as 600 targets simultaneously.

Its Hamilton Standard propellers are of mixed steel and foam/glassfiber construction, driven by a pair of 4910 shp (3661 kW) Allison T56-A-425 turboprop engines. Along with their C-2A Greyhound carrier-on-board delivery counterparts and a few remaining Grumman C-1A Traders, the Hawkeyes are the only propeller-driven aircraft still operating aboard US Navy carriers. E-2Cs have now been exported to Egypt, Israel, Japan and Singapore.

LEFT Yellowshirt FDO supervizes deck parking of a Grumman E-2C Hawkeye from VAW-126 aboard the USS *John F. Kennedy*.

BELOW AND RIGHT Despite its size, the E-2C's maximum take-off weight is less than that of a stores-laden A-6E or a 'clean' F-14A and poses no problem for the catapult – this one on the USS *John F. Kennedy*. Plane-guard SAR SH-3 helicopters aside, 'Hummers' are invariably the first aircraft to launch during flying operations and the last to recover. The Hawkeye's 2000 lb Randtron AN/APA-171 rotodome, colloquially known as the 'frisbee', measures 24 feet in diameter.

ABOVE This little piggy: orange razorback insignia on this sunset-splashed E-2C identifies it as the property of VAW-114, 'Hormel Hawgs'. Though not visible here, VAW-114 usually have a litter of tiny porkers running around the circumference of their rotodomes.

E2-C HAWKEYE

A VAW-126 E-2C lands on the deck of the *JFK*. The Hawkeye can also act as a 'memory' dump for the carrier's CAP F-14As AWG-9 radars, storing a Tomcat's 24 targets in its memory bank while the fighter is freed to acquire a further two dozen. Fuel and weapon status of F-14As can also be up- or down-linked to the E-2C's computers, enabling the Hawkeye's 'moles' – the air controller, combat information officer and radar operator who work in the dark confines of its fuselage – to deploy their forces most effectively. A typical Carrier Air Wing has a detachment of four E-2Cs.

E2-C HAWKEYE

BELOW An E-2C Hawkeye of VAW-124 'Bullseye Hummers' is catapulted from *Nimitz*. The pilot will fly a zig-zag pattern at low level to prevent an enemy AEW aircraft detecting his departure and thus giving away the position of the carrier.

ABOVE Taken from the island of *America*, an E-2C
of VAW-123 'Cyclops' displays its artistic rotodome.
The 'frisbee' can be fully lowered for the aircraft to fit
into the hangar deck. Before flight, hydraulics lift and
lock the dome to maximize radar performance.

LEFT E-2C Hawkeye of VAW-125 'Torchbearers'
tucks its wings away after landing aboard *Saratoga*.
During flight operations the Hawkeye is the first
fixed-wing aircraft to take-off and the last one to land.
The SH-3H rescue helicopter is the real early bird and
only lands after the last aircraft has been recovered.

LEFT Airborne early warning (AEW) is an absolutely critical part of a carrier's defences because even the most powerful surface radars can't see over the horizon. Without AEW, low-level strike aircraft can sneak in and cripple the carrier and other warships in the battlegroup with stand-off weapons such as sea-skimming anti-ship missiles (ASMs). Enter Hawkeye. The current E-2C 'MiniWACS' can automatically track at least 600 targets simultaneously and take automatic control of more than 40 intercepts and strike missions.

The Hawkeye's AN/APS-125 radar, manufactured by General Electric, is enclosed in a circular Randtron AN/APN-171 rotodome. There isn't enough space to accommodate a relief crew, so after a typical four-hour mission spent staring into display consoles in a dark, windowless compartment, the 'moles' tap down their helmet vizors before stepping out into the sunlight, ready to be led along the flight deck like little children crossing a busy road.

RIGHT E-2C of VAW-125 'Torchbearers' taxies out for launch from *Saratoga*. The E-2C is powered by two Allison T56-A-425 turboprops each rated at 4910 shp (3661 kW). Its Hamilton Standard propellers employ glassfiber to protect the radar from Doppler interference.

ABOVE E-2C Hawkeye of VAW-125 spreads its wings before being launched from *Saratoga*.

RIGHT The previous model: an E-2B Hawkeye of VAW-113 'Black Hawks' parked on the *Coral Sea* in July 1983.

BELOW A smaller 'Hawg' but a large sash were the colors worn by VAW-114 back in 1983. The Hawkeye squadron was embarked on the *Carl Vinson* during the carrier's inaugural world cruise.

BELOW The large island superstructure of the *Enterprise* towers over the co-pilot of an E-2 from VAW-117 'Wall Bangers' as he reads through his flight notes before the next mission. The colored bar under the cockpit is a squadron citation, and the 'Battle E' denotes efficient service over a set period of time.

The interior of the Hawkeye is not over-large when compared to the E-3 Sentry or the Soviet I1-76 'Mainstay', but then neither of these leviathans operate from a carrier deck. Although seemingly cramped inside, the five crew – pilot, co-pilot, combat information center officer, air control officer and radar operator – find the overall working environment perfectly tailored to their individual needs. The newer E-2s now entering service with the Navy are packed with the impressive AN/APS-139 advanced radar processing system (ARPS) built by General Electric, and an even more advanced ARPS with enhanced overland/overwater processing ability is due to enter service (and eventually be retrofitted into all fleet Hawkeyes) in 1991.

BELOW LEFT With its wingtip appearing to be too close for comfort from the parked Intruders ranged over catapult two, a Hawkeye from VAW-114 Hormel Hawgs rockets down the deck of *Carl Vinson*.

BELOW AND LEFT The pilot of a 'Hormel Hawgs' Hawkeye releases the arrester wire after landing back on *Carl Vinson*. Large power-operated Fowler flaps

and long-span ailerons slow the E-2 down before touchdown and also help the pilot to keep this large aircraft on the correct approach angle.

BOTTOM Another view of the same VAW-114 E-2C, side number 601, as the outer wings slowly begin to fold back. The large hinge skewers the outer wing panels round until they lie parallel with the fuselage.

E2-C HAWKEYE

BELOW A Grumman C-1A Trader, *Salt One*, catches the wire and comes safely aboard the *Nimitz*. The Trader is a derivative of the Hawkeye's predecessor in the AEW role, the E-1B Tracer. It's powered by two Wright R-1820 radials each rated at 1525 hp (1138 kW), and can take off without catapult assistance on *Nimitz*'s 4.5-acre flight deck.

RIGHT Although there has been talk of low-vizing E-2s, the squadrons have not yet been officially told to paint out their colorful badges and national insignia. As one Hawkeye crewman put it: 'If the enemy gets through to us then the F-14s haven't done their job and low-viz paint won't save us.' This Hawkeye has the old VAW-117 unit badge from 1983.

LEFT Allison T56-A-425 turboprops fired up, a Hawkeye from VAW-117 'Wall Bangers' awaits the arrival of its remaining crew members before being unshackled and directed out to one of the catapults. Inside the large rotodome perched on top of the fuselage is the aircraft's main 'weapon' – the General Electric AN/APS-125 airborne early warning radar. This system was retrofitted to the E-2 fleet from 1976 but it is now being replaced by GE's new APS-139 which is capable of tracking targets over land and sea at distances up to 300 miles from an altitude of about 30,000 feet. A useful adjunct to the Hawkeye's primary role is its ability to recognize and classify enemy electronic emissions.

RIGHT Close-up view of the fuselage of a VAW-116 'Sun Kings' E-2C Hawkeye.

LEFT The Trader's replacement, the Grumman C-2A Greyhound, began appearing on carrier decks in 1966. It has an obvious family resemblance to the Hawkeye but the fuselage is entirely new and can accommodate up to 39 passengers or 10,000 lb of cargo. Here a C-2A from VR-24 is almost ready to be boosted from the deck of *Saratoga*.

RIGHT It's not known at the time of writing whether the portly COD C-2s will succumb to the march of low-visibility markings in the US military. Hopefully, the doubly inaptly named Greyhound will continue to add a splash of color aboard American carriers.

BELOW The Greyhound carrier on-board delivery (COD) aircraft is a specially designed variant of the E-2 Hawkeye. This particular aircraft from VRC-50 (BuNo 162150) is one of 39 C-2s ordered by the US Navy to replace the remaining C-1 Traders.

CORSAIR SLUF stuff

The A-7E first flew on 25 November 1968 and deliveries began the following year. Unlike the earlier A-7A/B, the E-model is powered by a Allison TF41 (a license-built Rolls-Royce RB.168 Spey turbofan) which produces 15,000 lb of thrust. Other differences are a 20 mm Vulcan cannon and more advanced avionics: the A-7E was one of the first aircraft fitted with head-up display for the pilot.

A total of 535 A-7Es were built and despite the advent of the multi-role F/A-18 Hornet, the Corsair will remain a front-line aircraft with the US Navy well into the 1990s. The plane's nickname – 'SLUF' – translates into 'short little ugly fella' in polite company.

LEFT Carrying a 'buddy' refueling pod under its left wing, an A-7E gets a wave-off from the LSO and begins its bolter pattern for another attempt.

ABOVE Steam billowing from the bow cat, an A-7E is lined up for launch from *Nimitz*.

LEFT Jet blast deflector raised behind it, an A-7E of VA-81 'Sunliners' brings its F41 engine up to 100 per cent prior to being launched from *Saratoga* in August 1984. The VF-74 Tomcat in the background, side number 200, is assigned to commander of the carrier air wing (CAG).

ABOVE RIGHT Weathering of the low-visibility paint scheme is exemplified by this A-7E of VA-97 'Warhawks'.

RIGHT Incomplete national insignia and extended in-flight refueling probe distinguish this A-7E of VA-12 'Kiss of Death'. The Navy prefers to use the probe and drogue method of in-flight refueling rather than the 'flying boom' system used by the Air Force. Side number 400 indicates that this Corsair is flown by the CAG commander.

A-7E CORSAIR

A line-up of A-7Es aboard the USS *America* (CV-66) in July 1984. Side numbers 306/310 belong to VA-46 'Clansmen' and side numbers 410/401 are from VA-72 Blue Hawks.

A-7E CORSAIR

BELOW A VA-83 Corsair teamed with a KA-6D, the
tanker version of the A-6 Intruder, on *Saratoga's*
flight deck. Side number 523 is a US Marine Corps
KA-6D operated by VMA(AW)-533 'Hawks'.

ABOVE A VA-83 Corsair about to hit *Saratoga's* deck in the typically flat, no-flare landing attitude which gives a better view of the real estate during the approach and puts all the rubber on the deck at the same time.

LEFT This A-7E of VA-83 'Rampagers', equipped with a FLIR (forward-looking infrared) pod under its right wing, is directed to one of *Saratoga's* bow catapults. The Corsair can dangle an encyclopedic variety of death and destruction under eight hardpoints spread under its wings and belly: Rockeyes, Snakeyes, Walleyes, CBUs, rocket pods – you call, it hauls.

RIGHT A-7E Corsair, side number 407, of VA-81 'Sunliners', looking good for the number three wire on the rainswept deck of *Saratoga*. Landing lights are aglow to help the LSO (landing signal officer) monitor its approach in poor visibility.

A-7E CORSAIR

An impressive simultaneous launch of an F-14A
Tomcat and A-7E Corsair from the waist and bow
catapults of *Nimitz*.

ABOVE A Vought A-7E Corsair II of VA-82
'Marauders' in high-visibility markings is ready to
taxi to its parking space after being recovered aboard
Nimitz. The cockpit design of the Corsair bestows its
pilot with superb vision in the forward hemisphere
and makes the demanding task of landing the
airplane on a pitching, rolling carrier deck that little
bit easier. But the gaping nose intake is a positive
menace to deck crews and constant vigilance is
essential – being sucked into the engine can ruin
your whole day.

BELOW Newly painted A-7E, side number 307, of VA-82 'Marauders' is the nearest Corsair in this line-up on *Nimitz*, pictured in January 1983.

BOTTOM A-7E Corsair, side number 304, of VA-97 'Warhawks' in low-visibility scheme tied down on the USS *Coral Sea* (CV-43) in July 1983. The pilot's entry ladder is extended.

A mix of VA-82 Corsairs (nearest camera) and VA-86
'Sidewinders' with A-6Es of VA-35 'Black Panthers'
in the middle aboard the USS *Nimitz*.

TOP With its avionics hatch still open and the pilot's boarding ladder extended, this A-7E from VA-22 'Fighting Redcocks' is being turned around for its next mission. The AIM-9L Sidewinder missile mounted on the fuselage pylon gives the Corsair a self-defence capability against enemy fighters.

ABOVE The cockpit of the Corsair is tight but comfortable. Visibility is quite good out of the canopy, although the bulk of the ejection seat (a McDonnell-Douglas IG-3 Escapac) and the aircraft's broad fuselage spine severely restricts rearward vision.

ABOVE With his vizor down to block out the effects of the low morning sun, a pilot from VA-22 'Fighting Redcocks' looks out of his cockpit with a glance as menacing as the tip of his Sidewinder missile. Also visible is the HUD (head-up display) mounted atop the instrument panel. This particular aircraft, also pictured opposite, has a non-standard dayglo ejector seat warning triangle painted immediately behind the pilot's name.

A-7E CORSAIR

BELOW All-moving tailplanes angled firmly down, wings folded out and 500 lb Mk 82 bombs secured to the racks, an A-7E from VA-97 'Warhawks' is guided onto the catapult. The rather mottled appearance of the paint scheme is noteworthy. Although the 'cat men' are paid extra by Uncle Sam it seems a less than adequate reward for working in this intense, dangerous environment.

BOTTOM Bombed-up and ready to go, two Corsairs sit secured to catapults one and three on *Carl Vinson* while an F-14 is guided between them.

BELOW Launch! The pilot is pushed firmly back into his seat by G-force as his mount shoots from the deck of *Carl Vinson*. This particular Corsair is armed with retarded Snakeyes.

LEFT The arrester wire having scurried away after being released by the hook, this well-worn Corsair of VA-27 'Royal Maces' turns to prepare for parking. Its wing fold mechanism is already under way.

BELOW LEFT Corsairs also operate as tankers backing up the dedicated KA-6Ds. A large 'buddy' pack is usually mounted on stations one or eight, balanced by bolting two 300 US gallon Aero tanks under the opposite wing. This A-7E Corsair, side number 404 (BuNo 159288), from VA-27 'Royal Maces' is rigged with refueling gear and awaits its turn for launch from *Carl Vinson*.

The USS *Carl Vinson*, or '*Battlestar*' as she is known to the carrier's loyal crew, was until October 1986 the newest carrier in the Navy, but this honor now belongs to her sister ship, the USS *Theodore Roosevelt*.

RIGHT This is what the best-dressed A-7 pilots are wearing. The flight helmet is specially fitted and tailored to his individual needs and is decorated with the squadron colors (in this case VA-27 'Royal Maces'). The hose on his left breast connects with the oxygen system in the cockpit and also contains the microphone lead. On the other side of the suit is his life-preserver kit, which contains items essential to the pilot's survival should he be forced to eject or crash-land his aircraft. The tinted, double thickness vizor is especially clear to give the wearer an unobstructed view of the sky around him. The snugness of the G-webbing is clearly visible in this shot, the proliferation of zips and pockets also being distinguishing features. The suit is connected up to the aircraft's environmental control system through an umbilical cord once the pilot is strapped into his cockpit. The air bladders within the suit then inflate and deflate according to the manouver the pilot is pulling.

ABOVE LEFT The drabness of this Corsair is matched by the threatening skies in the background. Once a very colorful squadron, VA-22 'Fighting Redcocks' have now also succumbed to the disease which has afflicted nearly all operational aircraft in the Navy – low-visibility grays.

LEFT Now this is more like it! A far healthier VA-22 Corsair in the days when the 'Fighting Cock' was really red. Side number '302' is fitted with a forward looking infrared receiver (FLIR) pod underwing, used to improve the aircraft's night attack capabilities. The Navy only has 91 of these pods and they can only be fitted to 231 specially modified A-7s. The paint scheme is somewhat rare, being overall light gloss gray.

ABOVE An assortment of Corsairs from VA-22 'Fighting Redcocks' and VA-94 'Mighty Shrikes' parked under the gaze of the bridge on the USS *Enterprise* in 1983.

RIGHT A Corsair looms over the deck of *Enterprise*, poised for touchdown.

INTRUDER
Low-level
high-tech

The A-6 Intruder is a subsonic two-seat all-weather attack aircraft which began its US Navy career in February 1963. Intruder squadrons proved outstandingly successful during the Vietnam War – deep penetration missions against the North (often at night) produced good bombing scores and the aircraft became popular with its crews because of its inherent survivability. The program for the advanced Intruder, the A-6F, was canceled in 1988 to provide extra funding for the Advanced Tactical Aircraft (ATA), which will replace all A-6Es in the late 1990s.

LEFT A heavily weather-worn A-6E TRAM Intruder of VA-75 'Sunday Punchers' halts on *JFK's* catapult track to wait for the shuttle's return.

BELOW KA-6D Intruder of VA-34 'Blue Blasters' parked on the USS *America*.

A-6 INTRUDER

INSET, TOP With emergency procedures checklist and his 35 mm SLR camera stowed on the glareshield, this A-6E bombardier/navigator prepares to launch from *John F. Kennedy*.

INSET, BOTTOM All thumbs: fight deck officer and greenshirts give it the *Go!* signal.

BELOW Fly 1 beckons A-6E TRAM side number 505
onto the cat track aboard *JFK*.

LEFT Greenshirts look nonchalant as an Intruder goes off the *John F. Kennedy's* waist catapult.

BELOW LEFT A USMC 'Hawks' A-6E, nose gear strut extended, waits for the catapult shuttles tug which will accelerate it from zero to 150 knots in an instant.

RIGHT Greenshirt maintenance men attend to a 'Sunday Punchers' Intruder's capacious radome bay. The hemispherical fairing below the A-6E's nose houses TRAM (target recognition and attack, multisensor) equipment comprising FLIR, a laser rangefinder and tracker and spot designator in a radar integrated, stabilized turret.

BELOW Close parking aboard *Ranger* – A-6E TRAM of US Marine Corps squadron VMA(AW)-121 'Green Knights' nestles next to a Sea King helicopter.

BELOW AND RIGHT The wake of *Enterprise* forms an impressive backdrop as an A-6E TRAM Intruder from VA-95 'Green Lizards' lines up for a landing.

RIGHT 'Go that way'. The deck handler at right of picture directs an Intruder to its parking spot after recovery. The service life of the A-6E is being extended by fitting a new composite wing designed by Boeing.

LEFT An Intruder from VMA(AW)-121 'Green Knights', a Marine Corps squadron, hooks the wire and makes a textbook trap on *Ranger*.

BELOW A KA-6D tanker of VA-52 'Knight Riders' about to slam onto the deck of *Carl Vinson*. The old-style perforated airbrake from the A-6A sits immediately above the modification seen only on the tanker – the housing for the hose and drogue refueling line below the word 'NAVY'. The flap cut-out, a feature common to all Intruders, is also visible. Air-to-air refueling (AAR) is an integral part of flying operations; 'tanks' are used to extend the range or endurance of the fighters and attack aircraft and to save a crew from an early bath if their airplane is losing too much gas as a result of combat damage, a technical glitch or taking too many wave-offs in marginal weather with only 'bingo' fuel.

TOP An A-6E TRAM of VA-35 is manoeuvred for launch on *Nimitz*. The first A-6E TRAM flew in October 1974.

ABOVE Moments before launch, the catapult crew check the main breaker strut on the Intruder's nose gear leg. This VA-52 A-6E TRAM displays the red paint behind the leading edge slat, a marked contrast to the drab gray covering the rest of the aircraft.

ABOVE RIGHT Gear down, hook down, flaps down, slats out, air-brakes extended, a VMA(AW)-533 A-6E TRAM looks for the third wire aboard the *John F. Kennedy*. This aircraft is carrying a Sargent-Fletcher D704 'buddy' in-flight refueling pack on its centreline stores station.

CENTER RIGHT AND RIGHT In the groove: this A-6E TRAM is perfectly aligned for a textbook 'trap' aboard *JFK*. Note the Intruder's fully open split wingtip speed-brakes, adopted after trials with the Grumman A2F-1 prototype showed that rear fuselage dive-brakes disrupted airflow over the tail surfaces. Each carrier squadron has a landing signal officer (LSO), an experienced pilot who monitors and grades every trap made by his colleagues. There are four grades: *OK* (the naval aviator's way of saying excellent); *Fair*, not good, but safe; *No grade*, dangerous to pilot, other crewmen and aircraft; and *Cut*, so unsafe that a crash could easily have occured.

A-6 INTRUDER

BELOW The bombardier/navigator in the right-hand seat checks his mission notes as the pilot threads their Intruder towards the bow catapults of *Carl Vinson*. Side number 507 is bombed-up with four 2000 lb Mk 84s slung under a pair of multiple ejector racks (MERs).

BOTTOM A scruffy VA-52 Intruder returns to its parking spot aft. The A-6A entered US Navy service on 1 February 1963 and the first A-6E made its maiden flight on 10 November 1970.

BELOW The bombadier/navigator makes a signal towards the deck crewman (out of shot). This will be understood to mean, 'Arrester wire disengaged. Tail hook retracted. Aircraft rotating away.' The heavy weathering of the overall gray paint scheme on this VA-52 'Knight Riders' Intruder is typical.

BOTTOM Featuring an unusual yellow square marking on the left intake, this A-6E TRAM of VA-145 'Swordsmen' is securely tied down on the USS *Ranger*.

Inside the hangar deck of Saratoga: Grumman A-6E
Intruder, side number 500, of VMA(AW)-533
'Hawks' flown by the CAG commander is flanked by
an EA-6B of VMAQ-2.

A-6 INTRUDER

BELOW A weapons trolley carrying Zuni rocket pods waits in front of an A-6E of VA-65 'Tigers' in the hangar deck of *IKE*. Drop tanks are stowed up near the ceiling to save space.

RIGHT The Intruder is one of the most versatile aircraft ever operated by the US Navy. This A-6E TRAM of VA-145 'Swordsmen' has a 'buddy' refueling pack and two Snakeyes under each wing.

ABOVE High-viz, low-viz: contrasting tails of US Navy and US Marine Corps KA-6D and A-6E on the hangar deck of the *John F. Kennedy*.

RIGHT A-6E TRAM of VMA(AW)-533 in low visibility gray waits with tow bar attached on *Saratoga*. MERs (multiple ejector racks) are stacked on the weapons trolley in the foreground.

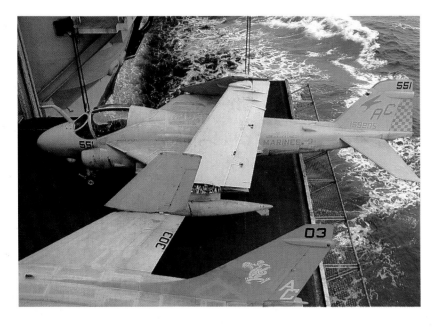

ABOVE A-6E Intruder side number 511, of VA-196 'Main Battery', pictured aboard the USS Coral Sea (CV-43) in July 1983.

LEFT Marine Corps' 'Hawks' A-6E TRAM on the side elevator of the *John F. Kennedy*. Six USMC squadrons fly the A-6.

ABOVE RIGHT A-6 bombardier/navigator of VA-35 'Black Panthers' gets his paperwork into shape before the pilot arrives.

RIGHT A-6E Intruder (BuNo 159570) of VA-196 parked on the *Coral Sea*. The bulbous nose radome houses a Norden APQ-148 multi-mode radar for simultaneous ground mapping, target identification, tracking and ranging.

BELOW VA-196 Intruders on the *Coral Sea* amid a tightly packed bunch of airplanes in July 1983. An A-7E Corsair of VA-27 'Royal Maces' is parked in the foreground, alongside an Intruder, with an F-4N Phantom of VF-154 'Black Knights' (since re-equipped with the F-14 Tomcat) to the rear. The current E-model Intruder first flew in November 1970 and is powered by two ultra-reliable Pratt & Whitney J52-8B turbojets rated at 9300 lb thrust which give it a maximum speed of 644 mph at sea level and a typical combat range of 1011 miles.

RIGHT KA-6D Intruder of VMA(AW)-533 parked near the fantail of a gale-lashed *Saratoga* behind an S-3A Viking and SH-3H Sea King.

BELOW Already hitched up to their 'mules', a trio of almost anxious-looking A-6Es wait to be towed out for launch aboard the USS *John F. Kennedy*. Again the conditions are hardly perfect – yet much of the time at sea, in contrast to the popular image, is spent operating in rain or poor visibility.

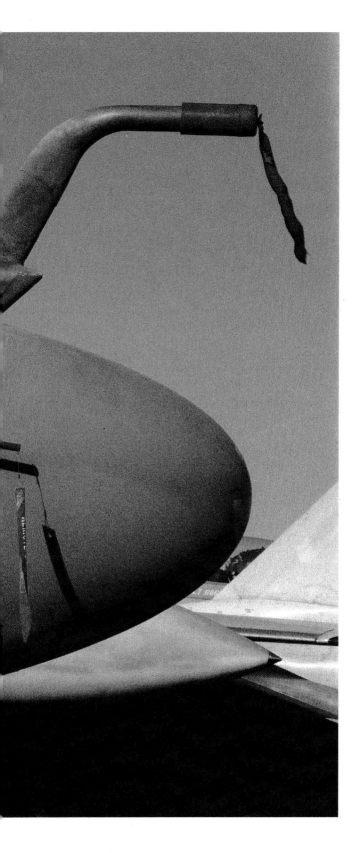

PROWLER
Beam weapon

Grumman's EA-6B is a four-seat electronic warfare development of the Intruder. The first Prowler flew in May 1968 and its ALQ-99 jamming system has been progressively upgraded to stay ahead in the 'battle of the beams' to neutralize or deceive enemy radars and communications.

LEFT A Prowler of the tactical electronic warfare squadron VAQ-136 'Gauntlets' on board *Ike*.

BELOW The Prowler's bulged fin-tip contains part of its extensive suite of ECM/ESM equipment; most of it is in special pods under the wings and fuselage.

Top left This Prowler from VAQ-131 'Lancers'
on the side lift of USS *Ranger* displays the gold-plated
canopies adopted as a crew protection measure
(unnecessary, as it transpired) against microwave
emissions from the ECM equipment and the threat of
cooking the crew in their seats.

Center left The EA-6B's jamming system is housed
in up to five external pods, three of which are carried
by this example from VAQ-136 'Gauntlets' embarked
aboard USS *Midway*, but seen here at NAS Atsugi in
Japan. A total of ten jamming transmitters can be
carried, each pod covering up to seven frequency
bands with simultaneous jamming in any two on
ICAP-2 (increased capability) versions of the Prowler.
The large fin-tip pod houses sensitive surveillance
receivers for long-range detection of radars.

Below left An EA-6B poised for a cat shot aboard
USS *Ranger*. This Prowler carries two jamming pods
and two 300 US gallon drop tanks. Tiny propellers on
the ECM pods windmill in flight to provide power via
a Garrett AiResearch ram-air turbine.

Below Pre-flight checks take the crew all over their
birds to ensure that nothing has been missed by the
greenshirts. This crewman, standing over the
mainspar of his Prowler, seems happy enough.

LEFT With the squadron colors of VAQ-134 'Garudas' visible on their helmets, the senior electronic warfare officer and one of his fellow EWOs keep a good lookout. The cockpits are crammed full of gear, with each EWO having a large panoramic video screen immediately in front of him. The senior officer operates half of the system's frequency coverage while the man behind him deals with the other half. The man behind the pilot is the third EWO: it's his job to jam the source of the radio and radar signals using the ALQ-92 and -99 systems.

BELOW Prowler '604' looking good for the third wire aboard *Carl Vinson*. The Grumman EA-6B Prowler represents the state-of-the-art in the design and application of airborne electronic warfare systems.

RIGHT The Prowler's main offensive weapon, the ANL ALQ-99 high-power noise jamming pod, hangs from the pylon underneath the wing hinge. The bulbous fairing on the fin contains several surveillance dishes, and more antennae are housed in the blisters further down the fin.

BELOW RIGHT Space is at a premium on the flight deck and aircraft are parked as close together and as near to the edge of the deck as possible. Prowler '604' seems to have been marshaled into a precarious position, but the deck handler has seen it all before and has the situation well under control.

EA-6B PROWLER

Prowler of VAQ-130 'Zappers' on the *Forrestal* with a rapid intervention fire vehicle in attendance. The radiation symbol on the nose helps landing signal officers (LSOs) differentiate Prowlers from Intruders when viewed head-on during landing approaches.

LEFT Affectionately known as 'The Whale', the Douglas EA-3B Skywarrior is an electronic countermeasures (ECM) platform packed with tons of sensors, decoys, jammers and assorted gismos to frustrate enemy radars and communications. Weighing a hefty 82,000 lb fully loaded, the EA-3B is easily the largest and heaviest aircraft to be seen on a carrier deck, but the roomy cockpit and its fine commanding view of the flight deck is appreciated by both pilot and navigator.

ABOVE LEFT At 72 ft 6 in the wingspan of the Skywarrior is wider than the F-14's in the fully forward position and this leaves little room for error on landing, even on supercarriers like *Carl Vinson*. The EA-3B is the only aircraft in the fleet which still uses the old bridle and brace wires system for launching.

ABOVE After a day's operational flying 'The Whale' from VQ-1 'World Watchers' is allowed to repose until the following morning. A small note inside the main landing gear door reads 'on loan from the Smithsonian Institute'. This airframe is a young one, built in 1958; the last new delivery (an A3D-2Q) occured in January 1961. This particular aircraft, (BuNo 146459), assigned to Air Wing 15, was unfortunate enough to get the blow-lamp treatment from an F-14 in full afterburner mode before take-off, which left her with a melted nose and bubbled window.

HORNET
All-round
stinger

McDonnell-Douglas's F/A-18A performs the same air-to-air/air-to-ground roles for the US Navy as the General Dynamics F-16 does for the USAF – only the Navy aviators would claim it does them better. As a fighter its Hughes AN/APG-65 multi-mode digital tracking radar can track ten targets simultaneously, displaying eight to the pilot. The Hornet featured strongly in President Reagan's retaliatory raids on Libya in April 1986.

LEFT VFA-131's 'Wildcats' took part in the 1986 Libyan raids. One of their F/A-18s is seen here aboard *Coral Sea* with Grumman A-6Es from VA-55 'Warhorses' in the foreground. The 'Wildcats' were the first Atlantic Fleet squadron to become operational with the Hornet.

BELOW US Marine Corps' F/A-18A squadrons share the attack role with their US Navy colleagues/rivals. Here a Hornet from MCAS El Toro, California-based VMFA-323 'Death Rattlers' – also Libya veterans – gets attention on the hangar deck of *Coral Sea*.

RIGHT A quiet moment for deck crewmen aboard *Coral Sea* amid parked Hornets from the two US Navy and two Marine Corps squadrons detached to the carrier.

LEFT This piratical F/A-18A artwork belongs to attack squadron VFA-132 'Privateers' based at NAS Cecil Field, Florida, and was photographed aboard the USS *Coral Sea* – the ship from which the squadron's Hornets were launched to attack Libyan targets in 1986.

RIGHT Air-to-air weapons for the Hornet include AIM-7 Sparrow, AIM-9 Sidewinder and AIM-120 AMRAAM missiles, while for surface attack the aircraft can carry AGM-65 Mavericks with a Martin Marietta AN/ASQ-173 laser spot tracker/strike camera and Ford AN/AAS-38 FLIR pod replacing Sparrows on the fuselage nacelle stores stations. AGM-84 Harpoon anti-ship missiles are also in the Hornet's weapons inventory.

RIGHT A brown-shirted plane captain puts some elbow grease into the cockpit area of a USMC VMFA-314 'Black Knights' Hornet aboard USS *Coral Sea*. Those big Navy-issue boots are great for foot protection but . . . they leave their mark on the lift-generating leading edge extension (LEX) strakes of the F/A-18A. Current dull finish low-visibility paint and toned down markings of US Navy aircraft are unpopular with pilots and deck crews alike, lacking the panache of the old semi-gloss light gull gray and white color scheme, whilst being more prone to heavy weathering and much more difficult to keep *looking* clean, even when spotless. That is, of course, all part of the camouflage experts' plan .

TOP Maintenance crewmen like to wear suitably decorated helmets to reflect squadron colors just as much as the pilot. Wearing the diamond stripes of VMFA-323 'Death Rattlers' on his cranial, a 'frog' listens to the deck directions being broadcast across the airwaves by the Air Boss.

ABOVE Stinging Hornet? Yes, indeed. This F/A-18A aboard the USS *Constellation* is from VFA-113 'Stingers', who must bemoan the passing of high-visibility colors when their bee insignia was more strikingly marked on A-7Es in black, yellow and red. The huge trailing edge flaps of the Hornet are at maximum 45-degree droop.

ABOVE A red-shirted ordnance man checks the wingtip AIM-9 Sidewinder station of a 'Privateers' Hornet aboard the USS *Coral Sea*.

ABOVE Equipped with ejector bomb racks, an F/A-18 Hornet from VFA-151 'Fighting Vigilantes' stands outside one of the hangars at the Naval Air Facility at Atsugi, south-west of Tokyo in Japan.

RIGHT With the Air Wing soon to embark on *Midway*, VFA-151 practice touch-and-go at Atsugi.

BELOW Hornet's sting? No, just the retractable in-flight refueling probe of an F/A-18. Unlike the USAF, which uses boom/receptacle flight refueling, the US Navy favors the hose-drogue method which enables non-dedicated aircraft such as A-6s and A-7s to serve as tankers using 'buddy' refueling packs.

LEFT The squadron badge of VFA-151 'Fighting Vigilantes' is a new design and bears no resemblance to the former multi-fin flashes which for many years adorned the tails of their F-4 Phantom IIs.

BELOW A Hornet from VFA-195 'Dambusters' (left) shares a parking space with its shipmate from VFA-151, also assigned to the carrier *Midway*.

F/A-18A HORNET

BELOW The F/A-18 is powered by two closely spaced 16,000 lb thrust General Electric F404 augmented turbofans. This VFA-195 'Dambusters' example is making its way back to the dispersal area after a routine training flight. Aircraft recognition experts will have spotted the Shinmeiwa US-1 search and rescue flying-boat, P-3 Orion and C-2 Greyhound parked in the background.

RIGHT This head-on view of the Hornet seems to reveal the aggressive 'sit' of this sturdy multi-mission strike fighter. Downstream of the radar radome is the central aperture for the muzzle of the 20 mm M61 Vulcan gun; the magazine holds 540 rounds. A neat retractable refueling probe is also situated in the tapered nose.

ABOVE A ground crewman checks fuel cell panels on a Hornet from VFA-192 'World Famous Golden Dragons'. The integral pilot's ladder swings up into the left LEX (leading edge extension) when not in use.

RIGHT Brightly colored helmet contrasting with his drab VFA-192 'CAG bird', Captain M. L. Bowman ('Badman') vacates his office after a mission. The Hornet has a large, comfortable cockpit and visibility is excellent.

LEFT Stormy skies, almost the same hue as the aircraft, frame an F/A-18 from VFA-195 . During their days as an A-7 Corsair II squadron, the 'Dambusters' were noted for their gaudy bald eagle markings which were emblazoned across the tails of unit aircraft. Now, however, squadron Hornets are far more conservative in color. The nickname 'Dambusters' stems from the Korean War, when an intrepid group of VA-195 aviators flew torpedo-laden AD-4 Skyraiders against the mighty Hwachon Dam. Needless to say the squadron completed their task .

BELOW An impressive line-up of 'Golden Dragons' on the flight-line outside CVW-5's hangar facilities. Hornet '310' has been temporarily grounded for extended maintenance – hence the aluminium foil over the canopy, wing rack and cannon muzzle on the aircraft's nose. The foil helps reduce moisture build-up in recessed areas, thus averting corrosion problems later in the aircraft's life.

BELOW, INSET Having just returned from a brief cycle of touch-and-goes on Atsugi's main runway, a VFA-192 pilot taxies his Hornet back to the squadron dispersal. Pilots usually select wing fold soon after vacating the main runway, a procedure completed as a matter of course on board the carrier.

VIKING
Sub-smasher

Lockheed's Viking S-3A anti-submarine warfare aircraft entered fleet service in 1974 and replaced the Grumman S-2 Tracker. Like the Hawkeye, it represents a brilliant exercise in packing an advanced weapons system into a relatively small airframe.

RIGHT The pilot of a US-3A COD Viking looks out through the heavily tinted windshield.

BELOW The 'Fighting Red Tails' aboard *Ranger* in 1982. This is the CAG's Viking, complete with rainbow colored fin tip and 'double nuts' zeros.

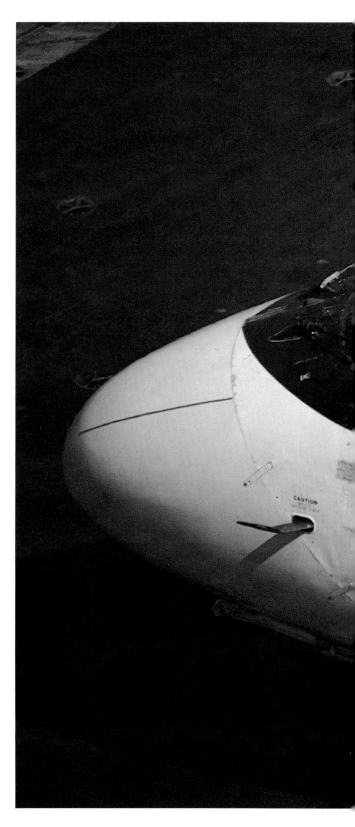

LEFT A VS-29 Viking(BuNo 160575) is forced to go around again because the deck is still obstructed by the last arrival. The arrester hook is locked down and the landing gear, based on the F-8 Crusader's, is also extended.

BELOW LEFT This time an S-3A Viking anti-submarine aircraft from VS-29 'Screaming Dragonfires' performs an impeccable landing on *Carl Vinson*. The aircraft will soon clear the deck for the next customer 30 seconds behind.

RIGHT The same aircraft, side number 705, comes to rest on the deck of *Carl Vinson*. Designed by Lockheed-California, the S-3 was a joint venture with LTV (Vought) which makes the wing, engine pods, tail and landing gear.

BELOW Not a pretty sight. Low-visibility S-3A of VS-29 'Screaming Dragonfires' waits for its crew aboard the *Carl Vinson*. The large wing hinges reduce the span by half and are skewed to allow the folded areas to overlap. Vikings are being steadily upgraded to S-3B standard, with new avionics and equipment and provision to launch AGM-84A Harpoon anti-ship missiles from the wing pylons. The internal weapon bays can accommodate four Mk 46 torpedoes, four Mk 82 bombs and various depth bombs or mines.

BELOW, INSET GO! The catapult officer points the way for an S-3A to take-off from the damp decks of *Saratoga* in August 1984.

BELOW Leaving a cloud of steam behind it, the Viking is catapulted off the carrier past Tomcats and Crusaders and into the gray skies.

ABOVE A VS-30 Viking unfolds its wings and waits behind a jet blast deflector prior to being launched from one of *Forrestal's* bow catapults. A VMFA-115 F-4S is lined up on the other bow cat in the background. Under a contract awarded to Lockheed in 1981 up to 160 Vikings are being updated to S-3B standard, introducing Harpoon anti-ship missile capability, a new sonobuoy reference system, better acoustic processing and enhanced electronic support measures (ESM). A retractable magnetic anomaly detector (MAD) is carried in the tail. The S-3 prototype first flew on 21 January 1972 and the first of 179 service deliveries of the aircraft followed in October the next year.

RIGHT Looking for the second wire, an S-3A Viking, side number 707 of VS-30, prepares to trap aboard the *Saratoga*.

BELOW The same airplane folding its wings. High-aspect ratio design helps to give the Viking a sea level endurance of some 7.5 hours. When the aircraft has detected a submarine it can kill it with torpedoes and depth charges carried in an internal weapons bay or mounted on underwing pylons.

S-3A VIKING

A flight deck officer from the *John F. Kennedy* is caught
in balletic pose amid catapult steam as he motions to
the crew of an S-3A Viking from squadron VS-22.
The wing-ports house ESM antennae.

ABOVE LEFT The 'Screaming Dragonfires' in all their former glory aboard the *Carl Vinson*. VS-29's splendid Viking boat motif has since shrunk to a smaller gray version.

LEFT Detail of a Lockheed S-3A Viking of VS-30 'Sea Tigers' aboard the *Forrestal* in July 1981. In addition to the dedicated anti-submarine warfare (ASW) version Lockheed also built one KS-3A tanker and six US-3A COD aircraft. Based at Cubi Point in the Philippines, VRC-50 operates a mixed fleet of US-3As and C-2A Greyhounds. Because of the large distances involved in flying out to the supercarriers of the Seventh Fleet steaming in the Western Pacific or Indian Ocean, VRC-50 is the exclusive operator of this fast, long-range aircraft. Due to the high cost of reopening the Viking production line (closed since 1980), this situation is unlikely to change unless new-build S-3Bs are ordered in quantity.

ABOVE Wings still folded on their machine, pilot and co-pilot go through their checklists before cranking up the Viking's two 9280 lb thrust General Electric TF34 turbofans. A tactical coordinator and a sensor operator sit in the aft cabin; all four crew have zero-zero ejection seats.

ABOVE An S-3 squadron usually numbers ten aircraft and they provide the primary anti-submarine force with SH-3H Sea Kings in support. These Vikings look smart in VS-21's traditional gray and white scheme, although their 'Fighting Red Tails' nickname rings slightly hollow today; the blood red lightning bolt which cut along the length of the fin (see page 170) has now been replaced with a lacklustre black outline.

ABOVE RIGHT A US-3A prepares to depart with a cargo of passengers, priority items and mail, with the wings just beginning to unfold. BuNo 157995 has two Aero 1D auxiliary fuel tanks mounted under the wing pylons.

RIGHT 'Miss Piggy' at rest: the fin is only folded if the aircraft has to be struck down into the hangar for maintenance.

KINGS & KNIGHTS
Rotor power

Originally designated HSS-2, the aptly named Sea King was the world's first fully equipped anti-submarine warfare (ASW) helicopter. Its sensor package includes radar, dunking sonar, sonobuoys (dropped in a precise pattern around the target) and a MAD (magnetic anomaly detector) 'bird' reeled out on the end of a cable to help get a fix on a submarine by detecting distortion caused to the Earth's magnetic field by its presence. Once located, the sub can be sunk by homing torpedoes or depth bombs carried along the sides of the helicopter. Now in its third decade of continuous service with the US Navy, the Sikorsky Sea King is a vital art of the Carrier Air Wing's ASW armory.

LEFT These low-visibility marked SH-3Hs recovering aboard the USS *John F. Kennedy* are from HS-7 squadron. The red and yellow 'colander' device protruding from the starboard sponson is the magnetic anomaly detector (MAD) 'bird'.

ABOVE An HS-4 Sea King about to recover back on the *Carl Vinson* after another ASW mission. The tail of the MAD 'bird' can be seen protruding from the end of the stabilizing float.

ABOVE RIGHT The Sea King became operational in September 1961 and has given the Navy outstanding service ever since. Like the earlier SH-3G, the current SH-3H is also an upgraded conversion from the SH-3A. The Sea King is to be replaced by the smaller SH-60B Sea Hawk, also made by Sikorsky, but meanwhile this HS-6 'Indians' example continues to fly from the *Enterprise*.

The first nuclear-powered aircraft carrier in the world, *Enterprise* was commissioned in 1961. In nearly three decades of eventful service the carrier has seen combat off North Vietnam and, more recently, has patroled in the Gulf of Sirte during the Libyan crisis, relieving other supercarriers in this politically sensitive area.

RIGHT The same plane-guard Sea King lifts off as another HS-6 'Indians' machine goes through a preflight inspection in the background. A Sea King has to be on station alongside the carrier before any launchings can proceed in case a crew is forced to eject during take-off or landing .

Top left An SH-3H Sea King anti-submarine warfare (ASW) helicopter of HS-14 'Chargers' receives attention before the flight-crew get aboard to start the mission.

Left Another HS-14 machine, but this time painted in dreaded low-visibility gray. Despite the flying-boat hull and watertight planing bottom, landings at sea are not part of normal operations, but these design attributes provide a fair margin of safety in the event of an emergency splashdown. Buoyancy bags are carried in the stabilizing floats.

Above Agility is a quality common to many maintenance men but working on helicopters can be especially demanding. This Sea King, and the one next to it, belong to HS-9 'Sea Griffins' aboard the USS *Nimitz*.

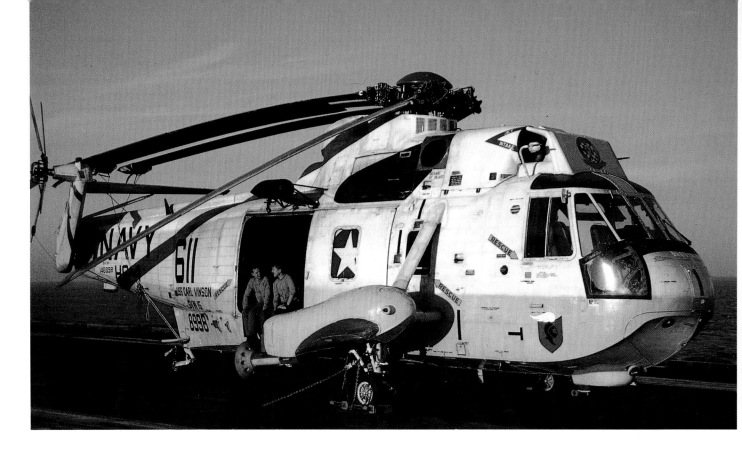

ABOVE The crew of an SH-3H Sea King rescue helicopter walk towards their machine across the rainy deck of the USS *Saratoga*. Its rotor blades and tail are still folded.

ABOVE LEFT An SH-3H of HS-4 'Black Knights' provides a convenient sanctuary for two greenshirts at the end of the day's flight operations. The Sea King detachment aboard ship usually numbers five aircraft and these machines are used in the general purpose utility role in addition to plane-guard and ASW duties.

LEFT All folded and stowed, a high-visibility (but grimy) light gull gray and white SH-3H from HS-17 shares the traditional helo parking spot in the shadow of *Coral Sea's* island with the ship's 'mule pool' of deck tractors. Sea King squadrons usually stake out their own territory beneath the bridge on every cruise.

The cargo-master guides his pilot down the deck of the *Carl Vinson*. This HH-46A Sea Knight is from Helicopter Combat Support Squadron Eleven and its Detachment (3) is flying from the Replenishment Oiler USS *Roanoke* (AOR-7).

LEFT In bright, if not garish, contrast to the drab field green 'Frogs' of the US Marine Corps, this US Navy HH-46A from Detachment 2 of Helicopter Combat Support Squadron Five (HC-5) is a positive riot of color. The star-spangled Sea Knight has just landed aboard the carrier USS *Enterprise* after a flight from its home ship USS *White Plains*. In addition to their routine stores replenishment duties, Sea Knights are the 'aerial mailmen' of the fleet, bringing welcome news from home for the 5000-plus crews of the supercarriers.

BELOW US Marine Corps helo pilots call their Boeing Vertol CH-46E Sea Knight twin-rotor helicopters 'Frogs'. A workhorse assault troop transport, a 'Frog' can carry 18 combat-ready troops or 4200 lb of cargo at a maximum speed of 135 knots. These CH-46Es are from HMM-161 squadron, seen here aboard USS *Tarawa*.

ABOVE AND TOP Cargo culture: an HH-46A from HC-6 uplifts lies for the USS *Coral Sea*. A crewman leans out of an open hatchway to check the security and stability of the underslung load.

RIGHT AND BELOW USMC CH-46Es performing their routine but vital task of ferrying men and supplies from USS *Tarawa* off the coast of Western Australia during Exercise Valiant Usher '86. Despite having only three legs, the Sea Knight really does look like a squatting Frog from some angles! USMC Sea Knights are likely to be replaced by Bell/Boeing Helicopter MV-22A Osprey tilt-rotor craft.

A Boeing Vertol CH-46D Sea Knight of HC-6
(Detachment 6) from the USS *Seattle* (AOE-3)
lands to deliver mail to the crew of *Saratoga*.

BELOW Stallion battalion: *Iwo Jima* class small assault carrier USS *Tripoli*, commissioned in 1966, is half the size of her *Tarawa* class cousins but plays an equally important role supporting US Marine Corps operations with the US Seventh Fleet.

LEFT, INSET Red-eye special. With its seven-blade 79-foot diameter main rotor and tire tail section folded, Sikorsky's CH-53E Super Stallion of HMH-465 poses less of a parking problem aboard the USS *Tarawa* than you might expect from a helicopter capable of carrying 55 combat-ready troops. Its three General Electric T64-GE-416 turboshaft engines total more than 13,000 shp, enabling the Stallion to lift all but the very largest items of USMC combat equipment. Maximum fuel range with the 1300 US gallon drop tanks seen here outboard of each sponson is 1120 nm, but this can be extended by in-flight refueling from USMC Lockheed KC-130 tankers. The bulbous projection on the starboard side of the nose is the retractable in-flight refueling probe. CH-53Es have successfully conducted in-flight firing trials of AIM-9 Sidewinder missiles, which could be provided for self-defence in combat situations.

PHANTOM Carrier classic

The **McDonnell-Douglas F-4 Phantom II** was *the* fighter aircraft for more than a generation, the benchmark design by which all others in its class were judged – and most didn't even come close. It is extremely unlikely that any Western jet combat aircraft will overtake the production total of 5201 racked up by the F-4 between 1958 and 1981, and none will ever match the kudos of flying in it. Even today, despite new high-tech hardware like the F16, F/A-18 and Mirage 2000, it's so good that at least three major aerospace companies are working on advanced versions, two of which (by the Boeing Military Airplane Company and Israel Aircraft Industries) involve transplanting its trusty J79s with Pratt & Whitney PW1120 turbofans.

LEFT F-4S Phantom of VF-74 'Be-Devilers' (now flying the F-14) being prepared for launch from the USS *Forrestal* (CV-59) in July 1981. The fairing on the intake is a radar warning receiver (RWR). The ultimate Navy Phantom, the F-4S is fitted with two-position wing slats to increase its manoeuvrability and a Westinghouse AN/AWG-10A radar with look-down/shoot-down capability. Installing 'smokeless' General Electric J79-GE-10B engines finally ended the 'follow the smoke and find the Phantom' jibes leveled at earlier Navy (and Air Force) versions. A total of 248 F-4Js were converted to F-4S standard.

BELOW Detail of F-4N Phantom of VF-154 'Black Knights' aboard *Coral Sea* in July 1983.

BELOW Detail of F-4N Phantom in low-visibility gray showing the extended in-flight refueling probe and ECM antenna.

ABOVE 'First in Phantoms' proclaims the fin of this F-4 from VF-74, and so they were. The 'Be-Devilers' received their Phantoms in July 1961 and completed carrier qualification trials on *Saratoga* in October that same year.

BELOW This VF-154 Phantom appears to have a form of wraparound camouflage under its left wing. The F-4N is a rebuild of the F-4B and features an improved structure, helmet-sight visual target acquisition system (VTAS), Sidewinder expanded acquisition mode (SEAM), a new main computer and one-way datalink. A total of 228 F-4B airframes were modified to F-4N standard.

ABOVE Detail of an F-4S Phantom of VF-74 'Be-Devilers' in light gray scheme.

LEFT An F-4S Phantom of VMFA-115 'Silver Eagles' – a US Marine Corps squadron. When this picture was taken in July 1981, VMFA-115 was assigned to *Forrestal*'s carrier air wing 17 (CVW-17) instead of the Navy F-4 unit VF-11 'Red Rippers'.

RIGHT AND BELOW RIGHT F-4N Phantom, side number 114, of VF-154 'Black Knights'. Its overall low-visibility gray scheme and subdued national insignia give the aircraft a drab appearance – a complete contrast to the vivid and colorful Navy Phantoms of the 1960s and 1970s. The close-up below reveals that at least one of its intake guards has been borrowed from VF-21 'Freelancers'. Two drone 'kills' are stenciled on the intake splitter plate.

BELOW F-4N Phantoms of VF-154 'Black Knights' (nearest camera) and F-21 'Freelancers' secured to the rear deck of *Coral Sea*. A crane has been swung out in the foreground.

BELOW Staying with the subject of splitter plates, this F-4N of VF-21 'Freelancers' aboard *Coral Sea* is wearing awards for excellence and safety – 'E' and 'S'. Many nations have flown the classic Phantom II over the past two decades, utilizing it as both an air superiority fighter and a bomb-hauling attacker. Over 5000 were built by McDonnell at St Louis, and 140 under licence by Mitsubishi for the Japanese Self-Defence Force, giving a grand total of 5201 bent-winged beauties! However, the aircraft was designed right from the start to a US naval requirement, its ability to perform all manner of tasks becoming legendary as the Vietnam conflict burgeoned. Powered by two trusty General-Electric J79s, and mounting an advanced (for its time) Westinghouse multi-mode radar in the nose, the overall package that became the F-4 Phantom II was

ideally suited for its multi-mission role. All things must come to an end, though, and the Phantom II was replaced by an even more remarkable aircraft, the F-14 Tomcat; so although the Navy was the initial operator of the F-4, it was also the first service to retire the venerable fighter. Its replacement, the Tomcat, is far superior to the Phantom II in every respect – from power availability to the searching strength of its radar.

RIGHT Camouflage begins to blend into the background as F-4J of VF-74 hurtles skywards from the deck of USS *Forrestal* on 2 August 1977. Under Commander Julian Lake, the squadron was one of the first to operate Phantoms in the early 1960s. Now, the 'Be-Devilers' fly the Grumman F-14A Tomcat. [*Photograph by Robert L. Burns*]

RIGHT In its disruptive camouflage scheme devised by artist Keith Ferris, F-4J of the 'Be-Devilers' of squadron VF-74 sits on the steam catapult of *Forrestal* (CV-59) in the Atlantic. Green-jacketed launch crew are part of the precision choreography which transforms a dangerous carrier deck into a functioning environment. [*Robert L. Burns*]

F-4 PHANTOM

BELOW Positioning an aircraft onto a catapult calls for the ultimate in co-operation between the pilot and the cat crew. Surrounded by suitably colored bodies, this 'Be-Devilers' F-4J is rigged to the waist cat on board USS *Forrestal* (CV-54). The blast deflector plate has been raised from its recessed position, and once the Phantom II is securely fastened to the catapult the pilot will test his engines. The leading edge slats give the aircraft more 'bite' into the airflow during the critical initial stages after launch. [*Robert L. Burns*]

RIGHT Virtually seconds from blast-off a 'frog' heads for cover after completing the pre-launch attachment between catapult and aircraft. His buddy is checking the tension of the wire brace on the port side of the F-4 and he too will soon vacate the scene. The system of braces and wires disappeared with the phasing out of the Phantom II. [*Robert L. Burns*]

BOTTOM Low-tech approach: an army of crewmen position AA-200 on the track. [*Robert L. Burns*]

LEFT A US Navy study concluded that experienced Phantom pilots reacted with greater apprehension to carrier deck landings than to battle with North Vietnamese MiGs. [*Robert L. Burns*]

RIGHT Parked beneath the gaze of the large, luminous number of the USS *Coral Sea* (CV-43), the sharp end of a VF-154 'Black Knights' Phantom II glints in the Mediterranean sunshine. Embarked on the trusty *Coral Sea* during the carrier's world cruise in 1983, the 'Black Knights' traded their tired F-4Ns for factory-fresh F-14A Tomcats soon after returning home to California, and with a swap in aircraft came a swap in carriers, the 'Black Knights' now cruising regularly on WestPac deployments on board USS *Constellation* (CV-64).

BELOW Its nosewheel at right-angles, AA-200 takes a breather on board USS *Forrestal*. [*Robert L. Burns*]

OVERLEAF: TOP LEFT F-4B Phantom (152269), side number ND-102, a distant visitor from the 'Devil's Disciples' of Reserve squadron VF-301 at NAS Miramar near San Diego, California, pauses at Andrews AFB, Maryland on 10 August 1974. Reservist pilots and radar intercept officers on Navy Phantoms were fully carrier- and combat-qualified and provided a powerful backup to regular aircrews in the Fleet. [*Joseph G. Handelman*]

CENTER LEFT F-4B Phantom (150993) of the Naval Missile Center at Point Mugu, California at the same base in February 1972, at a time when US warplanes were about to return to North Vietnam. [*Joseph G. Handelman*]

TOP RIGHT By 13 years later, as a precaution against visual and infrared sighting by latter-day enemies, aircraft markings had become so toned-down that only the black numeral 7 was easily readable on this NMC Point Mugu F-4S, Phantom in October 1985. [*Robert L. Burns*]

CENTER RIGHT F-4J Phantom (155529) of VF-171 at Key West, Florida, in 1981. [*James Rotramel*]

BOTTOM LEFT Bright red panels and tail emblem mark the Strike Test Directorate (STD) at NATC Patuxent River, or 'Pax,' in the Maryland tide water where naval aviators test airframes, equipment and themselves. F-4J Phantom (153839) is trailing its parabrake after landing at Pax in November 1978. [*Robert L. Burns*]

BOTTOM RIGHT Its companion 153768 differs in having the rear-fin radar warning and homing system (RHAWS) antenna found since the late 1960s on most Phantoms except reconnaissance models. [*Robert L. Burns*]

HARRIER
Vertical
venom

The US Marines Corps' squadron VMA-513 was the first to receive Hawker AV-8A Harriers in April 1971. Ten years later, flying the same aircraft up-graded to AV-8C standard with avionics up-dates, ECM gear, provision for triple ejector racks (TERs) on outer pylons and ventral strake lift improvement devices (LIDs), VMA-513 undertook their last operational deployment with the early Harrier before transitioning to the much more capable McDonnell-Douglas British Aerospace AV-8B Harrier II.

LEFT One of six VMA-513 AV-8Cs deployed aboard USS *Tarawa* for Exercise Valiant Usher '86 hovers above the deck prior to transitioning to forward flight.

BELOW The cramped cockpit and low profile canopy of the early Harrier illustrated here contrasts sharply with the big bubble hood of the new AV-8B.

Mission accomplished: a VMA-513 AV-8C pilot trudges to *Tarawa's* island for debriefing. While he is being debriefed and recounting tales of chasing kangaroos through the bush at low level, the various deck crew will be refueling the Harrier, checking its systems and then rearming it in preparation for the next mission. The turnaround time between sorties is kept to a minimum during exercises, the true professionalism of everybody involved being put to the test.

AV-8C HARRIER

USS *Tarawa* well under way with AV-8Cs, Bell
AH-1T Sea Cobras, Boeing Vertol CH-46E Sea
Knights and Sikorsky CH-53E Super Stallions ranged
on deck. Can you spot the sole Bell UH-1N Huey?

When Valiant Usher '86 was over, tired but trusty old AV-8Cs went into storage at the Aerospace Maintenance and Regeneration Center (AMARC, formerly MASDC), Davis-Monthan AFB, Arizona, while VMA-513 became acquainted with their new AV-8Bs at MCAS Yuma, on the Mexican border.

IN PORT

Life on board an aircraft carrier can be tedious at times, especially for the men who work below decks performing routine tasks that keep the ship functioning as a fighting entity. These crew members can go for days without seeing the sea or the sky, spending their time either at work or resting in a 12-hour on, 12-hour off shift arrangement. However, a sailor's lot is not entirely an unhappy one, for every 60 days or so the battle-group drops anchor in an exotic port for a week of 'R & R' (rest and recreation).

The Sixth Fleet, whose responsibility it is to 'police' the Atlantic and the Mediterranean, frequent some of the most picturesque ports during R & R stops: Monaco, Naples, Marseille, Nice, Port Said, Portsmouth and Hamburg are just some of the cities regularly visited by Sixth Fleet carriers. During the seven days in port millions of dollars are spent by the sailors and the US Navy also spends big dollars on foodstuffs, resupplying the gigantic galley stores on board the carriers.

The Seventh Fleet, which patrols the Pacific and Indian Oceans, usually spend longer periods at sea between port calls, but Fremantle, Mombasa, Manila, Singapore, Karachi and Hong Kong are the ports most often graced by the presence of its sailors.

LEFT The USS *America* was commissioned in January 1965 and in common with the other three *Kitty Hawk* class carriers she is powered by four Westinghouse steam turbines with a combined output of 280,000 shp (208,955 kW), giving a maximum speed of 33 knots.

During her 25 years of service, *America* has sailed predominantly with the east coast fleets of the US Navy, criss-crossing the Mediterranean on many of these cruises. Occasionally she is seen in the warmer waters of the Indian Ocean when the carrier is tasked to patrol 'Gonzo Station' in the Persian Gulf, or when funds allow the carrier to circumnavigate the globe. Unfortunately for the Navy, these 1960s-generation

carriers are powered by steam turbines and cost considerably more to operate than the slightly larger nuclear flat-tops. The ship displaces 80,800 tons and is crewed by 5380 men.

ABOVE The *Nimitz* class carrier USS *Dwight D. Eisenhower* is armed with approximately 95 aircraft and about half of them, gathered like nesting sea-birds, are parked on the flight deck in this view of the carrier in the picturesque Bay of Monaco. Seven different types of aircraft usually make up a typical air wing, although the *Midway* class carriers don't have the space to accommodate F-14s or S-3s. During a typical six-month cruise a carrier battle-group will visit three or four ports, usually spending seven days at anchor. While a vessel is in port only a small percentage of the 5000-strong crew remain aboard, a standard rota system being used to replace sailors every 24 hours. This means the entire ship's complement gets to experience the various joys of terra firma during the call. The ship may also be opened up for guided tours – a decision left to the discretion of the ship's captain.

ABOVE RIGHT F-14 Tomcat of VF-33 'Tarsiers' parked near the fantail of *America* with the hilly terrain of Naples in the background.

RIGHT Douglas EA-3B Skywarrior of the fleet air reconnaissance squadron VQ-2 remained aboard *IKE* when the carrier visited Monaco in June 1982. The Skywarrior is nicknamed 'The Whale' because of its shape and size.

The vast bulk of the *Dwight D. Eisenhower* on display in the port of Athens in March 1982. The carrier has an overall length of 1092 feet and a maximum beam of 252 feet; full displacement is 93,405 tons. Its two Westinghouse A4W pressurized water nuclear reactors can generate a total of 280,000 shp (208,955 kW) and give the carrier unlimited range and a maximum speed of at least 32 knots. Of its total complement of 6280, some 2620 are aviation personnel.

RIGHT Tomcats of VF-143 'The World Famous Pukin' Dogs' aboard the USS *Dwight D. Eisenhower*.

ABOVE An impressive mass of modern naval aviation hardware at rest aboard *IKE* in the Bay of Monaco. All belonging to Air Wing 7, the aircraft in this view include seven A-6E Intruders of VA-65 'Tigers', two EA-6B Prowlers of VAQ-136 'Gauntlets', two VF-142 'Ghostriders' F-14A Tomcats, three SH-3H Sea Kings, no less than 15 A-7E Corsair IIs from VA-12 'Clinchers' and VA-66 'Waldomen', four VS-31 S-3A Vikings and a solitary VAW-121 E-2C Hawkeye.

RIGHT While *IKE* rides at anchor off Monaco, a KA-6D Intruder of VA-65 'Tigers' is washed down to protect its aluminum airframe from the effects of salt corrosion.

The *Eisenhower* was the second *Nimitz* class carrier commissioned into service, the US Navy hoping eventually to have a total of six sailing the world's oceans. Because of their huge size (they are the biggest warships in the world) Navy carriers have to moor out to sea away from ports because they cannot physically fit alongside wharves. This means that small barges have to be lashed beside the towering vessels, and 'R &

R' boats then have to load up from these barges –
mean feat in a rough sea on an inking black night!
ke' is home-ported in Norfolk, Virginia – the
Navy's largest military establishment.

IN PORT

The USS *Coral Sea* anchored in the Bay of Cannes in July 1983. Commissioned in October 1947, an extensive modification programme included the installation of an angled flight deck, three steam-driven catapults and the relocation of her elevators. Crewed by 4560 men, *Coral Sea* displaces 64,000 tons and is powered by four Westinghouse steam turbines with a total output of 212,000 shp (158,208 kW), giving a maximum speed of 32 knots.